Praises For
Living in Balance

With Living in Balance, Christina Stern gently guides us to more fulfillment in our lives. The book is packed with the best of modern wisdom for caring for our minds, bodies and relationships, and delivered with the inspiring nudge we all need at times. Living in Balance offers so many clear ways to take small sustainable steps toward greater happiness, through asking us to pause and work with the strong amazing person we already are. I can't wait to share this amazing book with my students, clients and colleagues.
—Julian Pessier, Ph.D.
Director Stony Brook University Counseling and Psychological Services

Stern's "Living in balance," is a succinct guide to living a healthy life. A simple, approachable read with an intuitive layout— it can be easily navigated time and time again. It is precisely what makes a self-help book actually helpful. The "points to consider" sections offer great summaries of the focal points, which can even be used as personal mantras on the reader's journey towards improved mental health and balanced living. The final section on having a balance with others and maintaining overall balance is the real gem of the book. As Stern instructs: "Use the tools you have learned in this book when times are getting hard," and you will not be disappointed. The down-to-earth narrator creates a centering foundation upon which balance can be achieved in its raw, most honest form. Could Stern have tapped into the key to finding sustainable happiness even during one's darkest moments?

—Amy M. Negri, Ph.D.
Licensed Psychologist

In our fast-paced world that often feels like it's on fire, we could all use a little more balance in at least some parts of our lives. And if you're like me, and you're not sure where to start, the first step is picking up this book. Christina's focus on this aspect of bettering ourselves — finding balance -- is not only refreshing but also necessary. Whether it's with our thoughts, our relationships, or our bodies, Christina offers insights and tools to be healthier, happier, and more productive, in an informative yet accessible way. Just be prepared to put post-it's on nearly every page, because chances are you'll find yourself going back and referencing sections again and again. Mixing her real-life expertise with her own experiences, Christina makes you feel like you not only know how she incorporates balance into her own practice, but also into her own life. Christina isn't looking to preach her teachings and philosophies in *LIVING IN BALANCE*, but rather let the reader decide what works for them; by the end, you'll likely realize it can all be applied to your life, and you just might be better for it.

—**Jesse Lasky**, Author

Christina Stern presents us with a book written as if she is talking to each of us directly. Her ability to drill down to basic human experiences and feelings in a matter-of-fact manner is refreshing. The highlighted section summaries pull her commonsense recommendations together, offering practical guides to handling and/or reframing frequently experienced thoughts and emotions. The focus on balance in one's life allows Ms. Stern to focus the reading on a holistic approach to finding and maintaining stability in many areas of modern living and relating. Great resource!!

—**Barbara Sprung** PMHNP and Family Therapist

I was very excited to learn about Christina Stern's self-help book. I thought how wonderful it would be to have a "go-to" guide to help people make positive changes in their life. I completed this book in one day as it was an easy read and categorized into sections to help me stay focused. What I enjoyed most about the book is that Christina talks about real-life daily stressors and societal pressures. She also targets all distinct aspects that contribute to being a healthier individual (nutrition, physical exercise, positive affirmations).

As a therapist, I believe that books like this one can help people gain knowledge and understanding of how they feel. Christina made this book very relatable for all ages, and I also enjoyed how she shared her personal feelings and experiences. I would highly recommend this book for my clients and other professionals to read as it was informative and simplistic at the same time.

—Tara Sottile, LCSW-R
Clinical Director
Pathway Counseling, LCSW, PC

LIVING IN BALANCE

A simple guide to finding happiness and living your best life

Christina Stern

Published by KHARIS PUBLISHING, imprint of KHARIS MEDIA LLC.

Copyright © 2022 Christina Stern

ISBN-13: 978-1-63746-134-1
ISBN-10: 1-63746-134-8

Library of Congress Control Number: 2022938283

All rights reserved. This book or parts thereof may not be reproduced in any form, stored in a retrieval system, or transmitted in any form by any means - electronic, mechanical, photocopy, recording, or otherwise - without prior written permission of the publisher, except as provided by United States of America copyright law.

Scripture taken from THE HOLY BIBLE, NEW INTERNATIONAL VERSION ®. Copyright© 1973, 1978, 1984, 2011 by Biblica, Inc.™. Used by permission of Zondervan

All KHARIS PUBLISHING products are available at special quantity discounts for bulk purchase for sales promotions, premiums, fund-raising, and educational needs. For details, contact:

Kharis Media LLC
Tel: 1-479-599-8657
support@kharispublishing.com
www.kharispublishing.com

❝*For my children, may you always be kind, especially to yourselves.*❞

Contents

Introduction	vii
Having Balance In Your Thoughts	**11**
Low Mood	13
Anxiety	19
Anger	30
Feeling lonely	38
Self-Worth	41
Negative thinking	45
Expectations and Disappointment	49
Letting go of the past	53
Comparing to others	57
Having Balance In Your Body	**60**
Nutrition	61
Alcohol	68
Exercise	71
Sleep	74
Having Balance With Others	**77**
Finding balance with relationships	78
People pleasing	88
Difficult people	92

The world	98
Maintaining Balance	**100**
Gratitude	101
Coping	105
Goal setting	112
Time wasters	115
Take care of your things	118
Be kind	120
Be helpful	123
Keep practicing	125
About Kharis Publishing	129

Introduction

In my practice, I have spoken to many patients who are overwhelmed by daily life stressors and no longer know where to turn or how to make their situation better. Often people discuss feeling overwhelmed, stressed, depressed, anxious, or frustrated. Several patients report similar stressors and similar complaints. It is easy to become overwhelmed with the many demands we face in today's society. Balancing a career, family, and relationships can be an overwhelming task. I decided to write this book to discuss ways of managing these anxieties and coping with the stressors that many people in today's world experience. Maybe you are managing in life, and things are going okay. This book may still offer some helpful tools and tips to help you feel your best.

One of the important things I think we need to remember is incorporating balance in our lives. Be wary of letting something consume you. If you are hyper-focused on making large sums of money, you may be so focused on that one thing that other areas in your life suffer. Finances are important, but not at the expense of loving relationships, physical health, and self-development. Finding balance can be difficult for some people. Another example of not having balance can be in parenting. If you are always doing for your children and not scheduling any activities that you enjoy or caring for your physical health, it may leave you feeling depleted, exhausted, and unhealthy. Not caring for yourself and maintaining balance in your life does not benefit anyone, including those you love.

I will discuss ways to incorporate more balance into your life as we proceed. By having balance in multiple areas, you can feel a sense of control in a hectic lifestyle. When planning your goals, think about the many areas in your life that need tending to, including relationships, family, finances, home, self-care, and physical health. I want to help you create an overall balanced life that includes reaching goals in all areas. In my opinion, this is the path to happiness and self-fulfillment, which is achievable for all of us! Incorporating my time and family time may make a significant difference in your life. Becoming less of a procrastinator and working on time management may be the change you need.

I will be discussing ways to incorporate balance in multiple areas, including nutrition, relationships, and lifestyle. This book is categorized into four sections. Each section addresses an area that may block us from feeling our best. The first section is having balance in your thoughts. In this section, I address sad thoughts, anxiety, anger, loneliness, self-worth, negative thinking, expectations, letting go of the past, and comparing to others. These are the main themes I discuss when treating my patients. These include the thoughts that continuously revolve in people's minds and bring them down.

The second section is titled having balance in your body. In this section, I will discuss nutrition, exercise, and sleep. It is difficult to discuss overall health and wellness without addressing these essential topics. I consider these three items the foundation of well-being. If one of these areas is a problem for you, it may be limiting you from feeling good.

The next section is having a balance with others. In this section, I will discuss how our relationships with the people around us and our environment can affect our moods. People often view how the world should be and how people should treat them. I address these views and our expectations when interacting with others. I will discuss tools that can be helpful when dealing with difficult people.

The final section of this book is called maintaining balance. In this area, I will discuss tools that can be incorporated into your daily lives to help keep you in balance. In this last section, I discuss gratitude, coping skills, goal setting, time management, being kind, being helpful, and taking care of the things in your life. Keeping up with these areas in your life helps you maintain focus, have things that you can look forward to, and help you stay feeling good about yourself. I hope that this book can be a guide to help you learn ways to manage some of your stressors.

Having Balance In Your Thoughts

Low Mood

First, we will discuss moods. The chart below may be helpful when looking at where your mood is. Sometimes people are confused about where their mood is. They are not sure if they are feeling down or depressed. I have people come in for treatment and say they might be depressed, yet they are unsure. Keeping a mood journal can help you to determine where your mood lies. Below is an example of a mood journal. Tracking your mood will enable you to determine how often your mood is low and how severe the low moods are.

Monday	Okay most of the day anxious at night.
Tuesday	Mood was low in the afternoon. Anxiety at night.
Wednesday	Mood was good.
Thursday	Felt down most of the day. Crying throughout the day.
Friday	Mood was down most of the day. Anxious at night.
Saturday	Mood was okay.
Sunday	Mood was okay.

Everyone feels sad at some point in their lives. Sad things happen to us all. Feel your feelings; don't avoid them. Often, people feel sad and try to push away or avoid the sadness in hopes that it goes away. However, these feelings do not just disappear; they wait for us. The longer you avoid your feelings, the longer they will remain inside you. If you feel your feelings, you have a chance to move past them. By avoiding them, you ensure that they remain. Feelings are not good or bad, wrong or right. If you are feeling sad, then allow yourself to feel sad or cry. It is not a bad thing to feel sad. Crying can be therapeutic. I have spoken to people on the edge of crying but push the tears away and try to ignore the sadness. That is not coping.

It's okay to say you're not okay. It's okay to be sad sometimes. Sometimes, we feel like failures for admitting when we feel down or depressed in our society. We all feel down at times, and it does not make us failures. It is normal to have bad days. You may even feel down for weeks or months when going through some situational stressors. It takes courage to admit that you need help. Instead of viewing asking for help as a weakness, it can be considered a strength. By trying to do something about your sadness, you are being strong and not just ignoring it. You want to make your life better and take action. You deserve credit for acknowledging that there is a problem and being willing to work on it, and not ignoring it.

Depression is a deeper level of sadness. I ask my patients if they have a low mood or a depressed mood. There is a difference. Sometimes people feel low for a day or a few days, yet it does not mean that they are depressed. Depression may include feelings of hopelessness, inability to enjoy things, and difficulty completing normal daily tasks. This usually lasts for at least two weeks during cases of depression.

Depression can be so consuming that it can be hard to look outside yourself. You may be so consumed by your dark thoughts that you don't have room for anything else. Sometimes looking outside of yourself can help you to feel better. You may be focusing on how badly you feel over and over. You may be thinking, "I'm so depressed, I will never feel happy," or "Does anyone care about how I feel?" It's hard to move forward when your thoughts are just rotating about how badly you feel and what that is like for you. Try and think outside of the way you feel. Think about other things in your life or other people in your life. Take a moment to think of how the other people in your life may be feeling. Doing service for others can be very rewarding, and it can help us think outside of the depression or sadness that we are feeling. Finding a charity or a cause that helps others can be inspiring. This can help change your perspective on life and be a gratifying experience. Committing might be too much, but volunteering somewhere one day here and there may be possible. Even calling people and focusing on how they are doing might help you to change the focus on how you are feeling.

Suppose you tell yourself, "that won't help me. I don't want to go out; I'll just be miserable." In that case, these negative thoughts may be keeping you on a path of feeling bad. Something has to change to get better. Change is scary, but it's necessary. Make small changes. Small changes can be changing the foods you eat to be healthier, going for walks, getting out of bed during the day for short periods, or reaching out to someone when you are feeling badly.

Figuring out the reasons for your sadness can help you understand it and cope with it. What are the sad thoughts that go through your mind? Is there anger from past situations? Do you feel bad about yourself or your place in life? Becoming aware of what drives your sadness can help you understand it and make changes so that you can overcome it. Keeping a log of things that trigger your low moods and things that help you feel good can be very insightful. Determining what makes you feel down and what makes you feel good can be an essential step toward wellness. However, it can be hard to move past the depression without making any changes. In the following sections, I will discuss some things that bring us down and changes we can make to improve our mood.

Points to consider

- ➢ A mood journal can be helpful to see where your mood is most days.
- ➢ Allow yourself to feel your feelings and not push them away or ignore them.
- ➢ Acknowledging when your mood is down is a strength and a step in the right direction.
- ➢ Thinking of other people and how they are feeling can be helpful when your depression is consuming.
- ➢ Conquering depression usually involves change. Even small changes in your life, like cleaning your room, can be helpful.
- ➢ Try to learn what may be the reasons for your low mood. This can be a big part of curing depression.

Anxiety

Nearly every day, I interact with patients about their anxiety. Anxiety is something that we all experience regularly. In many ways, anxiety can help us. If we did not feel anxious about losing our job, we might not bother going to work and doing a good job. If a person has an upcoming exam, some anxiety can be normal and expected. During finals week, many students experience anxiety. Sometimes the anxiety we feel takes over our lives, which is when it is no longer helpful. Anxiety can be so overwhelming that people can begin to feel anxious about everything and anything. This can lead to a feeling of losing control.

I often think of anxiety as one's mind being stuck in the past or the future. People often become anxious about what may happen, "What if I get sick or hurt?" Sometimes people worry about things they did in the past, "Should I have said that?" or "Was that the right decision?" These thoughts can continuously loop again and again in your mind. The anxiety is not often in your present moment. It takes you to a different place in time, the past or the future. This is when I tell people to practice being in the present moment. Focus on what you are doing right now. Where are you? What do you see? What do you smell? What do you hear? You may tell yourself that you are home, sitting on a chair, looking at a picture. Repeat this to yourself to bring yourself to your actual place in time. Remind yourself that you are safe.

I try to have patients repeat to themselves, "I'm okay right now. I'm home, and my thoughts are making me anxious. Nothing bad is happening to me right now. All the bad that is happening is happening in my mind." It's important to bring yourself back to where you are—the present moment. You may need to repeat what you are doing at the moment to be able to be present. For example: "I'm home, and I'm about to eat lunch. I am taking out the bread. I am taking out the peanut butter. I am getting a plate." This may seem tedious, but with time it will get easier. This is one way to learn to spend more time in the present moment.

When your thoughts become too overwhelming, I encourage people to try to make things simpler. This can be done by getting closer to the present moment. For example, sometimes people emphasize a future event that may be a week or a month or a year away. Even though this is a future event, it may create a great deal of stress. Instead, I encourage people to focus on what can be done today or this week. If there is nothing that can be done for this event today, it is essential to acknowledge that. For example, if you are trying to get a job and have already submitted the application and are waiting for a response, there is nothing more that can be done at this time…

It is helpful to think, "Okay, I have done what I can for this, and there is nothing more I can do today. Time to focus on something else." Sometimes it can be helpful to think about what you can do this week for a future event. Once again, if there is nothing you can do about it, it's time to move on. Thinking about something you have no control over will bring you nothing but more stress. If there is something you can do to plan your event, it can be helpful to make that plan and write it out.

Sometimes people feel anxious about things like upcoming flights or trips. Unfortunately, these events do not have any tasks to help decrease their anxiety. In these situations, the only thing you can do is redirect yourself and distract yourself. You may need to continuously redirect yourself from the recurring anxious thought, and that's okay. Imagine the thought coming into your mind and passing like a cloud moving through the sky. It takes practice. If you can discuss the fears you have with a therapist, sometimes this can help to decrease anxiety levels.

Feeling overwhelmed can be a significant aspect of anxiety. Sometimes, people feel as though there is too much to do, and they do not know where to start or how they will get things done. People may feel overwhelmed about projects at school or work, household responsibilities, or managing finances. The list of things that can be overwhelming seems endless. When there is a big overwhelming task, it can be helpful to divide it into smaller, more manageable tasks. For example, it may seem overwhelming to plan a wedding, but it seems more manageable when you divide it into smaller tasks. This can apply to a school paper, a work project, or even purchasing a home. Finding ways to divide your task down into smaller chores will help you cope with the anxiety and pressure that accompany it. Try to focus on one task at a time. Look at only step one. Then when that step is complete, move on to step two. People often think of the whole staircase and feel completely overwhelmed.

I encourage people to write these tasks down in an organized manner. Being organized and making a plan can significantly reduce anxiety. For example:

Week of April 20th	Write Biology paper outline	
Week of April 27th	Complete rough draft Biology paper	Make study guide for English
Week of May 4th	Complete Biology paper	Review study guide English
Week of May 11th	Final paper due Biology	Final exam English

Sometimes, when I speak to patients about things that make them anxious, they have developed a story that may not be true. For example, a patient may explain that she made a mistake at her job and her boss looked at her badly. Now, she may be worried about getting fired and how she will pay her bills if she gets fired. She may even be thinking about other jobs she may be able to get when the firing happens. Even though it is just a story she has developed, this is happening to her. I tell patients it is like they have a puzzle to complete, and they only have a few pieces of the puzzle. The puzzle is far from finished, and they cannot make out what the picture will be once it's completed, but they are already trying to finish it without all of the pieces.

Think about what you know to be true when you start adding to your story or finishing your puzzle. I would talk to my patient about the things we know. She made a mistake at work. That is really all that we know. The look she may have thought her boss was giving her may not have meant anything. Perhaps, her boss could have recalled something he forgot or may have had an upset stomach. The rest is just her thoughts spinning down a rabbit hole and getting further from the truth. What are the facts? What do we know? Everything else is just our thoughts creating a story. Everything else is just trying to finish a puzzle without all the pieces.

It is often difficult for people to stop their obsessive thoughts, no matter how hard they try. Concerning these patients, I will discuss having break periods from these obsessive thoughts. It may be too difficult to completely stop the thoughts, but it might be more manageable to take a break from them. For example, if someone obsessively thinks about wanting a new job, the thoughts do not get them any closer to their goal. I will encourage them to have some time in the morning to reflect on that thought and then take a break. Say to yourself, "alright, I thought about getting a new job all morning, and I won't think about it again until tomorrow morning."

Sometimes, you cannot stop the obsessive thoughts, but you can try to pause them. If you cannot go until the following day, have a break until after lunch if you need. "Okay, I thought about that all morning, and I'm going to take a break from thinking about getting a new job until after lunch." Sometimes it can be helpful to even set a timer when taking a break from the thoughts. Allow yourself to reflect on your thought when the timer goes off. Then think about the thought and set a new timer to allow yourself a break. The thought may come into your mind, and when that happens, just think to yourself, this is my break time, and I will think about that again later or tomorrow morning.

You may feel like you are continuously redirecting yourself initially, yet it will get easier in time. With practice, this can improve, and you can reduce obsessive thoughts. This applies to many types of obsessive thoughts. For example, patients sometimes think obsessively about getting sick or going bankrupt. Whatever the thought may be, try to apply this principle and remember to focus on the facts. Is this a fact or a thought that I am worried about? Thoughts are not facts. Sometimes worries seem so real that they feel like reality even when they are just our thoughts.

People often feel anxious about things that they do not have control over. For example, they may worry about if they will get a job once they finish college when they are at the beginning of their senior year. These are thoughts that cannot be figured out at this time. When feeling anxious about something, consider if the problem you may be focusing on has a solution at this time. If it does not, thinking about it will only make you more anxious. This is when you tell yourself there is nothing I can do about this problem right now, and when I can do something about it, I will. Is there an action you can take about this worry? If the answer is no, then it is a problem with no solution. These problems tend to fester in our minds and make us feel more out of control because there is nothing we can do about them. These types of worries are "What if I get sick before my trip?" or "What if I am single forever?" We only have so much control over these worries.

You can wash your hands regularly and try having a nutritious diet to avoid getting sick, but there are only so many things you can control. If you are single, you can try to meet people, but there is no guarantee that you will find a life partner. So this is when you can only reassure yourself that you are doing what you can, but you do not have control over these problems. Focus on what you can control and the steps you can take to achieve your desired outcome. Just acknowledging the small things in your control may bring a sense of relief.

There is not a perfect solution for everything. Sometimes we just need to wait and see what happens and hope for the best. This is difficult for many of my anxious people. They want to know if problem A happens, then I can do this. If problem B happens, then I can do this. And so on. However, this is not realistic, and we cannot match a solution to every problem. Sometimes we just have to leave things unsolved. It would be so nice if we could find an answer to every problem and a plan for every issue. To have our problems neatly kept on a shelf instead of thrown in a mess.

Sometimes we must accept there is no neat way of fixing our problems, and sometimes there is a mess we cannot clean up. For example, if you are having issues with your boss and you are caring for a sick family member, there may not be a solution to these stressors. During these situations, you do the best you can and focus on the things in your control. Some things cannot be fixed or solved, but we can use the tools we have to help manage the stress. Using redirection can be helpful in these situations. Keep in mind that when you feel overwhelmed, this feeling will not last forever. There is a beginning, a middle, and an end to the anxiety. It usually peaks and then declines.

Points to consider

- Some anxiety is necessary for life.
- Practice being present.
- Think about what needs to be done this week, today, or this hour, whatever point in time is manageable and less overwhelming for you.
- Divide larger tasks into smaller, more manageable ones.
- Practice being organized and writing upcoming tasks down.
- Focus on the facts and don't add to the story.
- Take breaks from obsessive thoughts by distracting yourself or redirection.
- Try to determine if there is a solution to this worry. If there is no solution, practice moving forward.

Anger

>———•◆◆◆•———◄

People often come to me and report feelings of anger. They are unsure how to control their anger and lash out at people around them. If you are having difficulty managing your anger, I recommend taking a pause or walking away. If you are angry and unsure what you will say to people or do, this is the first step. Walking away from the situation will give you some time to relax and calm down. It may seem difficult at the moment, yet this is important. Often, people report feeling shame or guilt for things they said or did when they were angry. When you walk away from the situation, you can go for a walk, listen to music, do some deep breathing exercises, or maybe just scream into a pillow. If you are at work or at a place where you cannot just walk away, then take a pause. Pause your words and your actions temporarily. As difficult as this may be, it is the most beneficial thing to do in some cases. The anger and frustration will begin to settle once you give yourself some time.

When people hold on to anger, I try to understand why they feel angry. Where does the anger come from? If you are often angry with a family member, try to understand why. Is there a lot of resentment or unresolved past issues? If you are holding onto anger towards someone for things that happened several years ago, that anger only comes back to hurt you. Deal with the anger and resentment towards that person so that you can move forward and let the anger go. If the anger is not directed at one particular person and the person is angry with everyone they meet, I try to understand the reason for this. This anger has come from somewhere, and it is worth figuring out where it came from. Without understanding the cause, it can be difficult to cure the anger.

If someone is angry with many people they meet, something is likely within the person that is bothering them. It is probably not about everyone else. I interact with patients who are frustrated by most people they meet. I hear stories about anger towards family members, friends, co-workers, and anyone else that they speak to regularly. I attempt to understand the reason they feel angry with these people. Sometimes, I hear the following:

"They think they are so perfect."

"I know they look at me and think I'm fat."

"They think they are so smart, and I'm always wrong."

"They are so busy with their own lives and never make time for me."

When I hear these examples, I think about how it is more about the person who is angry than the other person in their life. Is insecurity the source of anger? Do they think people judge them, and does this cause them to become defensive or angry? Are they angry because someone else is successful, pretty, or in good shape? They may be upset due to being jealous of the other person's traits. If someone thinks they are perfect, does it really matter unless you feel like they are judging you? Why do you care? If they are rude to you or mistreat you, I understand, but being angry with someone because they believe they are perfect is just wasting your energy.

If you are angry at thin people, then this can be because you are unhappy with your weight. It really does not have anything to do with the other person. It is not their fault that you are unhappy with your weight, and it is not fair to be angry at people for their weight. If you know someone who knows a lot about everything, you might be annoyed by this, making you frustrated. But it does not really matter how much they know. That is not a reason to be angry with them. Do you feel like you know less when speaking to this person? Does speaking to this person make you feel bad about yourself? Once again, this depends on how you feel about yourself.

If someone acts like they know a lot, but they really do not, this can be sometimes difficult to tolerate. If someone thinks they know something that I know is not true, yet they continue to believe deceit, I just say, "okay." If I share my fact and they disagree with me even though I know that I am correct, I just let it go. Why do I care if they are wrong about something? If they do not believe me and want to continue to believe something that I know is not true, it does not affect me. It's not worth arguing with someone or getting angry with someone about small things. There are plenty of people that will tell you things that are not true or try to argue about their beliefs, but it does not really matter what they believe. If you are confident in your beliefs and feel good about yourself, then there is not anything that someone else can say that will get you down.

If you get angry with people for not paying enough attention to you or calling you, I wonder if this is due to a feeling of loneliness. Do you get angry with others for having other things to do? Do you feel like other people are living their lives and not bothering to include you? This can be upsetting, but this feeling goes back to your inner feeling of loneliness. It is not someone else's fault that they are busy. I understand the desire to want to be included and not want to feel left out of things. At such a point, I suggest looking at other things you can add to your life or do with your time. When others are busy, it should not become something that you get angry about. Find new things to do or other people to spend your time with. I understand that it can be disappointing if you have a friend or family member that you feel never checks in on you. If this occurs with someone that you really want in your life, then let them know that you would like to spend time with them more often. If you let them know and they still do not make time for you, then you have taken the action that you can take and do not have control over what they do. Focus on the people who make you feel good and show that they are there for you.

Sometimes people become angry about someone else's lifestyle. It can be difficult to understand someone that does not have the same values as you do. If someone has a different religion or sexual orientation from yours, this may seem wrong to you. I do not believe you need to change your values or agree with their lifestyle, but getting angry about it is pointless. People will have different views than you regarding lifestyle, politics, and religion but try not to allow these differences to cause anger and hate towards others that think differently. If the lifestyle or view that the other person holds is dangerous or hurtful to others, that is a different story, but if the person just believes something differently, it is best to let them have their belief and retain yours. If the person is interested in learning about your belief and is open to it, feel free to share your point of view with them. However, if they are not interested in learning about your belief, leading to anger and arguments, I recommend you let it go. It's important to let people make their own choices. As long as the person is not causing harm to themselves or others, you may disagree, but it's better to let it go. People need to make their own choices, even if those choices are mistakes.

Points to consider

- When you are angry, take a pause and walk away.
- Try to learn and understand your reasons for getting angry.
- If you are holding anger and resentment from past situations, try to get past them. Treat others based on how they are treating you now, not how they treated you ten years ago.
- Try to understand if you are angry because you feel judged by others or insecure about something.
- If someone else does not agree with something you are saying to them, even if you know you are right, just let it go. It

does not matter if they are right or wrong in most cases. So let them be wrong, and don't let this make you angry.

➢ If you are getting angry at other people's relationships or happiness, this can be due to your loneliness or unhappiness. It's not their fault. Instead, find ways that you can be more satisfied with your life or relationships and don't take these feelings out on other people.

➢ If someone engages in a lifestyle that you do not agree with, it is okay to disagree with this, but you don't want to feel angry about this. People have the freedom to choose a lifestyle that makes them happy even if you disagree with it. This does not make them bad people.

Feeling lonely

In our busy world, many people feel alone, surrounded by a sea of people. Loneliness is a trigger for depression. Some people report feeling lonely even when living in a house full of people or even when they are with their partner. Remember when you feel lonely that you are connected to others somehow. You are connected to someone in your life that cares about you, even if they are not good at showing it. Sometimes when people feel lonely, they become focused on that feeling and lose sight of the people they have in their lives. If you don't think that is true, then think about how you are connected to all of the other lonely people. Some people feel just as alone as you do. There is someone out there in this world sharing the same type of feeling that you are feeling. You are connected to that person in your loneliness and, therefore, not truly alone. I speak to so many people who report feeling alone, and I wish they could understand that so many others are out there feeling the same way they do.

I encourage people who feel lonely to connect with strangers they meet wherever they go. If you go to the supermarket, smile at the cashier, make eye contact, and offer a kind word. You can go to the library or the bank and see people and smile. This human connection is essential. When you are feeling lonely, making these connections can be helpful. Smiling at someone and having the smile returned helps us feel less alone. Reach out to people instead of waiting for them to reach out to you when you feel lonely.

Maybe there is someone that you have not spoken to in a while or a family member that you do not speak to often. These people will probably appreciate the call or text. If you spend much time alone, you may want to volunteer at a local food pantry or animal shelter. Spending a short time each week doing this may help you feel more connected. Sometimes, people feel relief from loneliness by getting a pet. This is not a solution for everyone, but it can be helpful for some. You may want to join a local meet-up group. I have recently heard of virtual groups where people have started to connect with others. Finding activities that you enjoy and can do by yourself can help you feel less alone. Maybe you will enjoy your solitary time when you are occupied with something you enjoy. Spending hours with your phone or browsing social media will not help with the feeling of loneliness.

"You are only lonely if you're not there for you." Dr. Phil

Points to consider

- ➢ You are not alone in feeling alone.
- ➢ Connect with others everywhere you go.
- ➢ Volunteer some time so you can connect with others in a positive way.
- ➢ Look for local meetup groups or groups online.
- ➢ Find things that you can do by yourself that you enjoy.

Self-Worth

What do you value? What do you want to be proud of? If you place great value on material things, have a busy social life, and look a certain way, you may find it hard to reach a point of feeling content and good about yourself that is long-lasting. What makes you feel proud, accomplished, or good about yourself? With materialistic things, there will always be another item to acquire. The satisfaction from materialistic objects is fleeting. This satisfaction is very short-lived and can lead to feelings of emptiness. Behind every purse or watch is another purse or watch. There are newer clothes, cars, or accessories every season.

If you value having many friends and being included in social events, it may lead to more loneliness when events get canceled, friends move away, or you feel sick and cannot go out. You don't want to define your value by the number of friends you have or functions you get invited to. Friends may change with time. When thinking of friends, think of quality instead of quantity. It's nice to be liked, but you do not want other people to determine your value.

If your value lies in how you look, this can also lead to unhappiness. So many people change how they look to feel better about themselves, only to learn that they are still not satisfied. I have seen many beautiful people who are unhappy with how they look. I have seen people in great shape unhappy with how their body looks. Feeling good about yourself goes beyond looks and clothing sizes. If you are not happy with who you are, dropping a clothing size may not make much difference. How you look in your 20s will be different from how you look in your 50s. However, some personality traits like being kind, caring for others, being a hard worker, or having a good sense of humor can last a lifetime. Think of what you value. What traits do you like about yourself? Who inspires you and why? What values do you admire in them? Thinking about the qualities you admire or like in other people can help you to understand traits or values that are important to you. This can help you determine what you may want to improve on for yourself. For example, if you have seen a pretty person who maltreats others, you may recall that looks aren't everything.

What are the things that you would like to be known for? What would you like to feel proud about? These are the qualities that improve self-esteem, self-confidence, and self-worth. Focus on what qualities you value. Maybe you would like to focus on being a helpful person, being kind, being a good friend, being a hard worker, being a lifetime learner, having a good sense of humor, being a polite person, being organized, being a good listener, or being someone who tries to be the best person they can be. These are the qualities that make us feel good about ourselves. Think of self-esteem as if it were a cake. These important core values can be the cake portion (the foundation) and looks or materialistic things can be the icing. The icing may help the cake improve, but it does not make up the most crucial part. Without the icing, the cake will still taste good and be enjoyable. If your happiness is all about the icing, there is no foundation there, and your cake becomes a puddle of mush.

Points to consider

- Figure out where you are placing your value.
- Look at personal qualities that you admire or can be proud of and strengthen these.
- Put less value on looks or materialistic things.

Negative thinking

Have you thought positive thoughts today? Sometimes our world can be negative. As we watch the news, it may appear that we have been trained to focus on the negative. Some of my patients are masters at finding the negative in every situation. Even when I try to remind them of positive things, they downplay the positive and focus on the negative things. It's easy to think negatively sometimes. You can go down the complaining road or the gratitude road. Every morning, we can wake up and have something to complain about if there is traffic, if it's cold outside, or if it's raining.

However, there are also positive things that happen to us every day. Yes, even you! Waking up every day, having food in your refrigerator, or having a job can all be things to be grateful for. I can go on and on. Positive thinking is about perspective. There is someone in a worse situation than you right now, and they wish they could be in your shoes. Over time, if you train your mind to see more positive things, it gets easier. Sometimes, this is difficult for people, and it often takes time and practice to have a more positive mindset. Have you had any positive thoughts today? I often ask the patient this question and hear, "no, I haven't thought positive thoughts in a long time." Being positive is a practice, and it gets easier over time. Try thinking three positive thoughts every day. Initially, this may be difficult, but keep it up.

One type of negative thinking is going to the worst-case scenario. Some people say, "bad things always happen to me." Remember, there are good outcomes too. My negative thinkers often automatically bring themselves to the worst-case scenario of any situation. They may say, "yeah, I got a promotion, but it will be more work," or "I'm going on vacation, but I probably won't even have a good time," or "I have time off from work, but I'll just be stuck doing house projects." People can find the negative in any situation. What if there is a good outcome? I try to remind people that things may work out and

Living in balance

that there are other possible outcomes. What if you enjoy yourself on vacation or are happy to get that house project over with? Continuously focusing on how things will turn out bad before they even start is exhausting and will always bring you down. This is a sure-fire way to have a bad day every day. Try to think about the possible positives, even if it may seem difficult initially.

You must train your brain to cease thinking negatively in all situations, and the only way to do so is to discipline yourself to think positively. Thinking about a possible positive outcome might be a good first step. Merely thinking of a "maybe" scenario where things work out. Try to hold back your negative thoughts when speaking to people. If what you want to share is negative, try to just let it go. Think of what you are saying and if it's helpful or nice. If you are talking to others and complaining or saying things that are not nice, just let it go. If you are frequently focusing on negative things or complaining, I'm sure the people in your life notice this. If you are less negative, you may notice your relationships improve. People might enjoy speaking to you more often if you minimize complaining and negativity. Consider being more positive when commenting or posting on social media as well. Think about if the post you are about to share is negative and if it will make people feel bad or if it will be helpful and make people feel good. Over time, you may notice you are not working so hard to force yourself to be positive.

Points to consider

- ➢ Remind yourself to think of positive things every day. Even if it is something small.
- ➢ Are you going to the worst-case scenario in many situations? Think of what some good outcomes may be in every situation.

Expectations and Disappointment

We have so many expectations about what life should be and how we should be. Release your expectations; they are not helpful. Sometimes, you need to accept what is and let go of what you think it should be. People get so stuck on how things should be and not how things are. If you are always fighting your reality, you will always be at war with it. It is not helpful to think about what your relationship and family should be like. How can you make the best of what you have?

We have these expectations about ourselves as well. People expect a lot from themselves; these expectations can often be overwhelming and make people feel so disappointed in themselves that they give up trying. For example, I hear single people saying that they feel as though they should be married. I speak to people that do not have children, and they sometimes feel bad about this and feel like they should have had children. People speak about their careers sometimes and feel as though they chose the wrong one. The list of things people think they should have or should have done differently is endless. These expectations just make us feel bad about ourselves.

Stop trying to be perfect. You are only human. You will make mistakes, and it will be okay. People feel overwhelmed, thinking they are not a good enough parent, not a good enough student, not a good enough employee, etc. If there is a score to life, it's okay to get a B. It's okay if you are not getting A's in every area. You try the hardest you can, and that needs to be enough. Working all day and keeping your home tidy, and cooking nice meals every night alone can seem daunting. Sometimes, the house is not as clean as you want it to be, and some nights you may have to order take-out, and that's okay.

You don't have to be great at everything. People look at social media or read magazines about having a clean house, fancy looks, or a perfect-looking family, and they feel like failures. Don't judge yourself based on social media, television, or magazines. These cause unrealistic expectations. This same principle applies to the activities that we enroll our children in. We don't have to enroll them in many extracurricular activities for them to be successful or for us to feel like good parents. It's okay to be okay. Let them play. If they are not enrolled in any extracurricular activities and they are happy, that's a success in my book. I try to render the best service at everything. I can't be great at everything, and I'm okay with that. If I put too much pressure on myself to be better at everything, I would become overwhelmed and frustrated and feel like a failure. When you take a moment and evaluate yourself, chances are you are doing great.

Maintain balance in the different areas of your life. If you are spending all your energy on your career and doing a great job in that area, you may feel you are falling behind on your health, home, and family. If you feel like you have not put in much effort in certain areas of your life, make a plan to improve those areas. Take it slowly and focus on one thing at a time. For example, if you feel you have not been an attentive friend or partner, don't get stuck in the past. Instead, focus on where you are presently and how to make improvements. Maybe you will make more effort to spend time with the ones you love regularly. Every day is a fresh start, and there are ways things can improve without beating yourself up about it.

Points to consider

- ➢ Recognize your expectations and release them.
- ➢ It's okay to make mistakes and not be perfect.
- ➢ Try to maintain balance in the important areas in your life and not put all of your energy in one area and let the other areas go.

Letting go of the past

So often, people are focused on their past, which keeps them feeling sad. They feel stuck in their past and cannot move forward. If you are driving along a road, you can't move forward if you only look at your rearview mirror. You have to look ahead and look at where you are. Your past can either trap you or propel you to move forward. I have heard adults of every generation discuss childhood memories that have been difficult to deal with. Sometimes we need to discuss these memories to process them and move forward.

Unfortunately, some people use these memories as a reason not to move forward, and that is when it is unhealthy. If I hear someone in their fifties say their current relationships are failing because their father was cold and unsupportive, this is a block that has prevented them from moving forward. I hear people say they felt unloved in childhood, which has affected all of their relationships, and it is why they are unhappy and alone. I have also heard people say that because their parents did not teach them how to be independent, they cannot keep a job or be successful in life. Do you have any blocks that you are holding onto from your past that prevent you from moving forward and being the best you can be? Learn what the blocks are and acknowledge them. Think of the things that are in your control. Instead of focusing on the past hurts, think of what you can do to make your life better. Discussing these past hurts can help you to move forward. Even though it may be difficult, don't let your past determine your future.

You can only blame others for so long. At some point, your life becomes your responsibility. You cannot continue to blame others for your place in life. Maybe you had a difficult childhood. But it will not benefit you when you are forty years old, stuck in anger and blame, still holding on to your difficult childhood. I have seen this time and time again. You need to move forward and start making your own choices and taking responsibility for where you are in life. Yes, you may have had a difficult upbringing but make room for a new chapter in your life. If you focus on the past parts of your life, it becomes difficult to welcome the new ones that might be better. You may be unable to turn the page and be open to new possibilities if you hold on to the past.

Sometimes people have so much anger towards others. People feel angry about a friend who offended them many years ago or a lost job. Instead of moving forward, they complain about these things in life that have set them back "Oh, if only this worked out, I would be in a better place." And they are left continuously thinking about the experience or relationship that went wrong one, five, or ten years later. That experience happened and ended; it cannot be changed, and there is no going back. It's time to be where you are and think about how you can make your current situation better. Focusing on who wronged you in the past will not bring any satisfaction to your life. It will only rob you of your happiness and keep you stuck in a loop. It's hard for better days to come when you only focus on your saddest or most difficult days.

Points to consider

- ➢ Determine if your past has blocked you from moving forward.
- ➢ Discuss past hurts so that you can move forward.
- ➢ Let go of blame and anger from past situations.
- ➢ Think of where you are now and how you can improve your current situation.

Comparing to others

I often hear people compare themselves to others. This is never helpful. If you compare yourself to a neighbor with a bigger house or a nicer car, you will feel bad about yourself. In reality, that neighbor will have someone else who has a bigger house than them or a nicer car than them. They are in the same situation. Keep in mind that there is someone with a smaller house than you, a more beat-up car, or maybe no car. You aren't better or worse than anyone else. We are always in the middle in some way. Maybe someone has a bigger house than you but not as many good relationships as you. There is no way to fairly compare ourselves to others. We don't know how someone is feeling or what is happening in their lives. So the person whom we may think has it all may be struggling in silence.

I often hear people talk about how seeing photos or posts on social media make them feel bad about their lives. They feel like other people have great relationships and seem to have so much more fun or nicer things than they do. I remind people that photos posted on social media are not always depicting reality. Some couples constantly argue, yet post photos that make them look very happy together on social media. Just because something looks great on social media does not mean it is real. Someone can even post a photo of themselves with a filter that makes them look completely different. It's easy to get caught up in the glamour of the social media world, but this would be like comparing your real life to a movie that you watched on television. The only person that you should be comparing yourself to is you. Am I doing better than a year ago or a month ago?

Be happy for other people's successes. When your neighbor gets a new car, be happy for them. Instead of feeling jealous or angry, just try to feel happy for them. When people in your life make accomplishments, celebrate with them and acknowledge those accomplishments. Practice being a cheerleader for other people. We feel better when we celebrate people's accomplishments as opposed to being annoyed by them. Remember that you would want others to celebrate your accomplishments.

Sometimes, people tell me that they have a hard time when others are the center of attention. They report having difficulty when someone else is celebrating something or is the focus of attention. People explain that they may feel jealous or angry when other people do well. They do not want to feel this way but cannot help themselves. I tell people to keep in mind that we all have our turn as the center of attention. So it is that person's turn at that particular time, and it will pass. It will be your turn again; you will celebrate something or have an accomplishment that other people recognize. So let them have their time and remember that your time will come again, and at that time, you will want others to be happy for you.

Points to consider

- ➢ Comparing to others is never helpful.
- ➢ There is no accurate way to even compare to others.
- ➢ You can only compare yourself to where you were yesterday.
- ➢ Try to celebrate other people's success.

Having Balance In Your Body

Nutrition

It is difficult to figure out what to eat in society today. There is so much contradictory information that it is hard to figure out what food is good for us and what food is not. The food we eat is the fuel we are putting into our bodies. Lack of the vitamins and minerals your body needs can make you feel depleted, fatigued, and exhausted. There is also a connection between our diet and our ability to focus. I'm sure you have noticed that you may begin to feel moody, angry, and on edge if you have gone a long period without eating. We often dismiss the importance of the foods we eat. When we eat unhealthy food, we may say, "I know this is terrible for me, but it's just so good." Part of feeling good everyday is eating healthy foods.

It is not always easy to cook super healthy meals regularly, so I am encouraging you to use balance with your diet. If most of your meals are unhealthy, you can start by adding some healthier meals to your diet. Changing every meal daily may not be possible, but even little adjustments can help. Begin with one meal per day and gradually build up. Strict diet plans are often difficult to follow and stick with for long periods. I encourage you to change how you eat based on your lifestyle and what works for you. If there is a particular diet that you like and that works for you, I suggest you try it. Some people are successful when they follow a meal plan; others need flexibility and prefer a list of foods they can eat whenever they want.

Making healthy eating a lifestyle can help you in the long run. Maintain balance in your diet. Eat foods that are high in carbohydrates in moderation. If your plate is made up of mostly carbohydrates for every meal, like many people these days, your diet is not balanced. Some foods high in carbohydrates include pasta, bagels, bread, muffins, cookies, and cakes. Eating a healthy diet can help ensure you get an adequate level of vitamins and nutrients that your body needs to function. If you are not getting appropriate levels of vitamins like Folic Acid and Vitamin B-12, it can lead to lower mood and energy. It is hard to feel good when your mood is low at baseline and when you feel sluggish throughout the day. If your diet is unhealthy and lacking nutrients, no matter how hard you try to have a positive outlook and stay active, this may be challenging.

I suggest adding more healthy foods to your diet. Try to eat foods that have fewer ingredients and are more natural. Incorporating a good amount of vegetables into your diet is important. Often, people do not eat many vegetables at all. Vegetables can give a lot of vitamins and nutrients. Foods like brown rice, beans, legumes, vegetables, and fruits are healthy. The majority of the foods I eat contain simple ingredients. This helps to keep my diet uncomplicated and straightforward. If your diet mainly consists of fast food, try to reduce it. If you eat fast food five times per week, try to cut it down to two days per week and go from there. Prepare a sandwich for lunch instead of ordering out.

Unhealthy foods are overly processed. I try to avoid processed foods as much as I can. The longer something can sit on a shelf, the less likely I will eat it. But do I occasionally enjoy processed foods? Yes, I do because I try to maintain balance. Our diet cannot be perfect all of the time, but we do our best. Eating whole natural foods most of the time and incorporating processed foods in your diet sparingly can help you maintain a healthy diet for your lifetime. Maybe you can plan for a week or month that is free of processed food.

Another thing in our diet that should be limited is our sugar consumption. This includes artificial sugars. Eat sugar in moderation. One type of sugar that we should always avoid is high fructose corn syrup. This has been found to have adverse effects on our health. High fructose corn syrup has been added to so many foods that we eat. I suggest reading food labels to ensure the foods you are eating are free from high fructose corn syrup. This unhealthy ingredient has even been added to a lot of the bread found on supermarket shelves. If you have sugary drinks like soda and juice multiple times per day, try to reduce your intake. That would be a bonus if you could cut soda out of your diet.

I know many people really dislike water, especially if they are used to drinking sugary juices and teas throughout the day. If you are one of the people that drink much juice or iced tea during the day, consider mixing your juice/tea with water. Start with adding a little water, then gradually increase the water content and decrease the juice. Adding lemon juice to your water may make it more enjoyable. This can be a good start to decreasing your sugar consumption. Sugar is addictive, and it may be hard to decrease your sugar intake when your body is craving it. As you reduce your sugar intake, the cravings decrease.

When speaking to people about their diet, I also consider caffeine intake. If you have several cups of caffeinated beverages per day, this can lead to increased anxiety, restlessness, and poor sleep. If you are used to drinking several cups of coffee or tea during the day, how about switching to decaffeinated drinks after your first cup? Energy drinks should also be taken with caution. I have spoken to people who drink energy drinks throughout their day and feel they need them to get through the day. However, they have spikes and dips in their energy level throughout the day and do not feel energized. If you feel like you need energy drinks, there is probably something causing the low energy level that needs to be addressed. How is your diet?

Are you sleeping well? Have you had a physical? There are probably other healthy ways to improve your energy level without having energy drinks. Energy drinks may not be helpful if loaded with caffeine, sugar, and artificial ingredients.

Keep in mind that when looking at the diet you are eating for overall health—not eating to fit into a certain size of clothing or be a certain weight. When you base your eating goals on healthy living, you can never go wrong. Some people may look like your ideal size on the outside, yet it does not mean they are healthy on the inside. Eating right should be to maintain a healthy body. Focusing on that goal helps keep some of the added pressure and expectations from dieting. If you eat more healthy whole foods and decrease processed foods, sugars, and fried foods, you will reach your goals in time without following a strict diet plan.

Points to consider

- The foods we eat affect our mood every day.
- Start with adding healthy meals to your diet.

- Don't overdo the carbohydrates.
- Eat vegetables every day. Try to get 40%-60% of your plate covered with vegetables.
- Eat more whole foods.
- Reduce fast food intake.
- Decrease processed foods.
- Limit sugar intake.
- Eliminate high fructose corn syrup.
- Decrease sugary drinks.
- Drink more water.
- Decrease caffeine intake to 1-2 cups per day.
- Eliminate or limit energy drinks

Alcohol

Drinking moderate amounts of alcohol daily can cause depression, weight gain, and medical problems like cancer and liver disease; this is just a fraction of some of the adverse results drinking alcohol can have. If you want to feel your best, it may be hard to reach that goal if you drink excessively. The standard limit of alcohol is one drink per day for women and two drinks per day for men. However, I would recommend drinking less than that, for example drinking alcohol 2-3 days per week and having 1-2 drinks on the occasion you are drinking. It is okay if you drink more some weeks, but I would try to keep the alcohol intake close to this amount or less most weeks.

Sometimes people rely on alcohol to help with their stress. This can be a slippery slope. Some people can enjoy alcohol in moderation, and some cannot. Maybe you can enjoy a glass of wine with dinner every night and not have any issues. Some people have difficulty knowing their limits. Some people are problem drinkers. Do you become overly emotional when you drink or start fights and arguments? Do you blackout and forget events that happened when you were drinking? Do you have difficulty limiting the number of drinks you consume on each occasion that you are drinking? If you drink and wake up worrying about what you may have said or done when you were drinking, then you may want to work on this. If you need to call out of work due to having hangovers, then I would suggest you look at the amount of alcohol that you are drinking.

Even if you only drink once every few months, yet on the occasion that you drink, you black out, get in fights or arguments, or do things that you regret, it is essential to acknowledge that you may be a problem drinker. It is something to think about because many problem drinkers I speak to do not actually realize they are problem drinkers until we explore their drinking behaviors together. You may not need to stop drinking altogether, but you may want to watch your behavior and make some changes. For example, I have spoken to people that feel more depressed, have difficulty sleeping, and feel fatigued after a weekend of drinking.

You may be self-medicating if you are drinking heavily due to stress and anxiety. Maybe it is time to speak to someone about your stressors or your drinking. Regularly drinking heavily will not add anything beneficial to your life. It will not make you a less anxious person or a happier person. If you would like to decrease your drinking, add positive coping skills to replace the alcohol. It is more challenging to take away a negative coping skill and have nothing to replace it with. So maybe you can start exercising, doing puzzles, or cooking instead. We will discuss positive coping skills in a later chapter.

Alcohol interferes with sleep. I hear many people tell me that alcohol helps them to fall asleep; this may be true, but alcohol does not help you stay asleep. Alcohol may cause you to get less restful sleep and cause increased awakenings during the night. So if you are having difficulty with sleep, you may need to reduce alcohol intake, and you may see your sleep begin to improve.

Exercise

I know this one may be hard for some of us, but exercise has proven beneficial. Numerous studies have proven the benefits of exercise. Exercise is helpful for our physical and mental health. Exercise has been shown to help with depression, focus and concentration, and self-esteem, among many other things. If you live a sedentary lifestyle, I do not expect you to start running laps at your local track. Start slow. If you do not ever exercise, maybe begin with a 15-minute walk three times per week. You can increase that to 20 minutes, then 25 minutes, then 30 minutes. Aim for at least 30 minutes of exercise four days per week. Begin with something that can be attainable and long-lasting. If you start with an overwhelming routine, you may feel disappointed and stressed out, which will make you want to quit. Start slow and build from there. Remember that this is something you want to incorporate into your lifestyle for the long run. If you get off track for a few days and fail to meet your weekly goal, try to get back on track the following week. If you miss a few days or a week or two, it does not mean you failed, and you need to give up on exercising. Maybe it's time to try a different type of exercise or change your routine but don't quit. Exercising two times a week is better than zero times.

If you can find an enjoyable activity, it may not even feel like work. There are a lot of different forms of exercise to try. Many exercise videos can be found online, ranging from kickboxing, yoga, tai chi, weight training, and Zumba. There are also groups of people who engage in bike riding, walking, hiking, rock climbing, and running, which may be enjoyable. Exercising in a group may be more enjoyable.

Points to consider
- ➢ A sedentary lifestyle can lead to decreased energy and poor sleep.
- ➢ Exercise has been proven to improve our mood, energy level, and overall health.

Living in balance

➢ Start an exercise that you enjoy and are likely to continue.
➢ Reach for a weekly exercise goal.
➢ Exercising with others may help you to reach your goals and stay accountable.

Sleep

I can't stress the importance of sleep. If you are not sleeping well, it affects your mood, anxiety, and energy level. People who have a change in their mood or anxiety level often report sleep problems that have accompanied them. If you are having trouble sleeping, your body is trying to tell you something. Are you stressed? Maybe you need a new mattress. I had a patient who reported difficulty falling asleep and staying asleep for over a year. He tried different sleeping medications and decided to get a new mattress. After getting his new mattress, all of his sleep problems were resolved. This is probably an uncommon case, but it's a reminder to explore the cause of your sleep problems. If you cannot determine the cause of your sleep problems, you may want to consult with a sleep specialist.

Living in balance

I have some patients who stay up late at night and wake up late during the day, which has negatively affected their mood. Practice good sleep hygiene. Only go into bed when you are tired. Do not hang out in bed throughout the day. Turn off electronics before bed. Eliminate or shorten daily naps if you are having trouble sleeping at night. Avoid caffeinated beverages after lunchtime. Decrease alcohol intake in the evening. Keep the room cool and dark. Try a sound machine or meditation before bed. There are many meditation videos or apps that can be helpful. Keep a consistent time that you go to sleep and wake up. Try not to go to bed too late. This can be a difficult habit to break. If you are going to bed late, try to wake up at a decent time and avoid any daily naps. For example, if you wake up at 2 pm, set the alarm for 1:30 pm, then 1 pm, and gradually move the time earlier until you reach a healthier wakeup time. You may be able to regulate your sleep pattern to a better sleep and wake-up time. Some people sleep so late that they miss so much of the day. It helps your mood to sleep at normal times.

Points to consider

- Try to figure out the cause of your sleep issue. For example, is it stress, anxiety, caffeine, electronics in bed, or alcohol intake?
- Practice healthy sleep hygiene.
- If you cannot get your sleep on track, you can consult a sleep specialist.

Having Balance With Others

Finding balance with relationships

Having friends and family in our lives is essential, but at the same time, it can be a stressor for many. Sometimes our relationships can be toxic and can cause us pain. For example, if you live with someone who makes you feel worthless or shameful, it can be difficult to escape the constant negative environment. There can be a part of you that loves this person but another part that dislikes them so much that you feel at war with yourself.

Learning how to interact and communicate with these individuals can be helpful. Sometimes the best way to interact with these people is to give yourself more space from them. People often feel guilty when they take space from certain family members. I speak to parents who often feel their adult children are their biggest stressors and overwhelm them with their needs.

It's important not to put the needs of others before your own continuously. If you are feeling stressed with a family member that is overly negative or continuously drains you, it is okay to speak to them less. You are not doing anything wrong by taking some time for yourself. Some toxic family members can make you feel guilty for taking some space from them or setting limits.

Sometimes family members or significant others can push your buttons and may bring out the worst in you. If there is a person in your life who always makes you angry, which causes you to yell and say hurtful things that you regret, it's important to make changes in the relationship. Maybe it is best not to discuss topics with these family members that often cause tension. Sometimes we argue about the same thing with people repeatedly with no changed result. In some situations, there is a compromise that can be reached, and in other situations, there is not. It's important to be aware of when the situation cannot be improved and when it must be accepted. It is just better to avoid arguing with some people. These people usually escalate disagreements, do not accept responsibility, shift blame, and act like victims. If there is not something you can do to make things better, accepting the person and their stance is the best move. It does not mean that you agree with them or that they are right. It just means you are not going to change their opinion, and it would be better for you to accept it and find a way to live with it for your well-being. You may just want to say, "Okay, I understand that's how you feel about it, and I feel differently." If you are engaged in a conversation with this person and become angry, it may be better to take a break to avoid saying something you may regret. If possible, go to another room or step outside to give yourself some time to calm down. You may even need to go into the bathroom for some privacy. We will speak more about dealing with difficult people in the upcoming section.

I often speak to patients about how their family or friends make them feel. Sometimes, patients report not feeling important to their friends and family. When people are feeling down or lonely, they often feel this way, as though they are in a dark pit and no one is around to throw them a ladder and help them out. Often, family and friends care about our feelings yet are unaware of how to help us with them. For some people, when they see a loved one that is depressed or anxious for an extended period, they become frustrated. It is not always easy to help a struggling person. They may think, "what do they want from me?" It is easier to avoid the person or avoid discussing feelings if it seems too hard. This does not mean they do not care. It might mean they do not know how to help you.

I have been told that initially, family members may try to be helpful or offer a suggestion, such as, "just don't think about it," which is not helpful at all. If that does not work, the family member may become frustrated or angry that they are not getting over it. It's hard for people to understand how we feel, and it's even harder for people to help us out of our depression or anxiety. People begin to feel helpless. They want to offer a solution that will help us, but most of the time, they are unable to do so. It's hard to watch someone you love hurting. This often makes the sad person feel even sadder. They feel like they are a burden and should just be able to get over it, but they can't. It's not your fault for feeling sad. It's just how you feel. There is nothing right or wrong about it. Remember that your family members mean well, and they just don't know how to help you.

Often the people in our lives are so consumed with their own lives and feelings. They may not even be aware that we struggle, but we cannot accuse them. Sometimes we expect people to know how we feel when that is impossible. The people we care about cannot read our minds. You may think, "they should just know I'm feeling bad." Sometimes we give them clues that we are down and expect them to figure it out. But that's not fair to them. It is better to be direct with people and let them know how you feel or what you need rather than waiting for them to figure it out.

Many people in today's day and age are very busy and do not take the time to think about how other people in their lives may be feeling. They may be working on just trying to keep themselves together. We don't really know how other people feel, and we can't always expect them to help us out of our pit of depression. In many situations, other people cannot help us out of our pit as much as they may want to. Usually, the only one that can help us out of our pit is us.

Living in balance

It is not beneficial for us to wait for someone else to save us from sadness. People often do not know how to make us feel better, and we can't put that responsibility on them. Would it be nice for people to check in on us and tell us that they care? Of course! But to expect it from people can lead to disappointment. The people in your lives may not even know you are struggling, and we can't expect them to know unless we share our feelings with them, which can be difficult.

At some point, your friends and family will disappoint you, and you will disappoint them. Friends and family have disappointed me throughout my life. There were times I hoped someone would be there for me, and they were not. There were also times I was expecting someone to call me or visit me, and they did not. I thought some people would be more involved in my children's lives, but they were not. Once I started thinking about it, I thought there were probably times when people were disappointed by me, and I didn't even notice. There was probably a time a friend was hoping I would go out with them, and I was not in the mood to go out. Probably a time when someone was feeling down and was hoping to talk, but I didn't answer the phone. Also, there was probably a time when someone was hoping I would offer to help them with a task, and I did not. You're only human, and so are they. This does not mean your friends are not really your friends. Sometimes when we are disappointed by people, we think, "I thought they were real friends, but I guess they are not." If someone lets you down, it doesn't mean they don't care about you. It just means they are human. Give them time, and they may make it up to you.

This doesn't mean that it is okay when you have friends who take advantage of you and mistreat you. If people are mistreating you, they are not indeed your friends. However, when friends do not meet our expectations, it does not always mean they are bad friends. There are different levels of friendship. Some friendships are fun and casual but not very deep. Understanding the type of friendship that you have can be helpful. If the person is more of a casual friend, it may lead to disappointment if you expect more from them and want the friendship to be on a deeper level. It does not mean you are not friends; it just means the friendship is casual. Maybe they won't call you every day, and you will only hear from them once every few weeks or months; this is not an intentional way of harming you. Maybe they are not very social or may have many things keeping them busy in their own lives.

We feel all sorts of emotions regarding family members and friends. It's essential to stay in control of our feelings. Remember not to let anyone have the power to control your emotions. If a family member makes us angry, it's not necessarily the family member making us angry. Only we have the power to do that. If you haven't spoken to a boyfriend after a fight and feel depressed, remember that emotion comes from you. Of course, we will have emotions, and the people we care about will affect those emotions. Just remember that the emotions come from you.

Sometimes people say, "my boyfriend makes me so depressed" or "my mom makes me miserable." Try to take back the control of your emotions. It's not healthy for someone to make our lives miserable and have that much control over us. That is when we need to re-evaluate and take back our power. If your partner makes you feel so depressed, then assess the relationship. In what ways does your partner make you feel depressed? Maybe you need to work on your self-confidence. Maybe you need to step out more frequently and add other people to your life because you spend too much time together. Maybe you can work on the communication in your relationship to make it better. Maybe the relationship is not healthy for you.

Points to consider

- It's okay to have space from people if the relationship brings negativity or makes you feel down.
- If an argument is not going to result in a compromise and will just escalate, it may be better not to engage.
- If you find yourself having trouble calming your anger, try to go to a private place where you can relax.
- You can't expect people to know when you are upset or angry if you don't tell them.
- We can't expect people to make us feel happy. We have to do that ourselves.
- Often, people do not know how to make us feel happy when we feel bad, and they

feel helpless, which may lead to them feeling frustrated.
- ➢ We are all humans, and chances are, we may disappoint each other at one time or another in long relationships.
- ➢ Try not to put expectations on friendships.
- ➢ We have the power over our emotions; other people do not.

People Pleasing

Many people who visit me are people pleasers. They often feel this need to make other people happy with them. They go out of their way to please everyone else so that people do not get mad at them or disappointed. They sometimes feel guilty when they do not do things that other people want them to do. Being a people pleaser often leads to anger, frustration, and resentment. You become fed up with people expecting so much from you. Often, people feel unappreciated and taken advantage of. Remember, it is okay to say no. Suppose you feel frustrated and taken advantage of; try to take a step back and think about if you are doing things because you want to do them or because you feel as though you need to do them. Are you doing things for yourself or other people? It is nice to go out of your way for people when you can and when it feels good. But if you are going out of your way for people every time, and you feel they do not appreciate it and it's making you angry, then maybe it's time to stop. Do things when you can. Don't always put yourself last. It's important to fulfill your own needs too. There is nothing wrong with that, and you do not need to explain yourself to anyone.

It is okay if some people do not like you. No matter how hard you try, there will be people that do not like you. It does not mean you are not likable. Some people will not like you, and it will have nothing to do with you. You can't please everyone. You may be too loud for some people or too nice for some people. Believe me, I have heard people complaining about how people are too nice or too friendly. Maybe you have even heard people complaining about a superficial trait someone has and using this as a reason not to like someone. For example, "they dress weird, they have bad teeth, they look funny, etc." Some people do not like others because of their economic level, sexuality, or skin color. In my opinion, these are not reasons to dislike someone, and it informs me more about the person judging someone else based on these factors than it informs me about the person being judged. If someone does not like me because of the way I dress or my weight, they are not really someone I would want to have in my life anyway. Think of someone well known that you admire and I'm sure you can find critics of that person. We just cannot expect everyone to like us.

So many people want to be liked and try to change their personalities to be liked, but no matter what they do, that person will not like them. Instead of feeling bad about it or stressing out, keep in mind that this is part of life and will happen. If I meet 100 new people tomorrow, out of those people, some of them will not like me, and it may have nothing to do with me. So instead of focusing your energy on those who do not like you, focus on those who like you. If you get a vibe from your friends that they do not like you, try to meet new friends. Don't abandon your current friends; just add more people into the mix, which may help you feel better about yourself. Take a moment to decide if YOU even like that person. Maybe you don't even like them at all.

Points to consider

- People pleasing can lead to anger, frustration, and resentment.
- Do things because you can, and you want to.
- It's okay if someone does not like you. No matter how hard you try, not everyone will like you.

Difficult People

We will all come to a time when we deal with someone difficult. These people challenge us and make us feel bad about ourselves. Don't let difficult people change who you are. You may find yourself making rude comments or giving the person dirty looks. If the difficult person is rude or mean that makes them look bad. But if you join and start acting that way towards them, you also make yourself look bad. Don't let someone else's behavior influence your behavior. If you are behaving in a way that is not who you truly are, it's time to make changes. Try not to let others have that much control over your responses or emotions.

I like to let difficult people be the teachers in my life. They can help to teach me patience. Whenever I am dealing with a difficult person, I try to let it be an opportunity to work on myself.

I let this be a time to practice being calm around those personalities. I think it helps me to be stronger and more resilient.

Don't argue with someone that won't get it. If you have a person in your life that argues with you about things and never makes an effort to understand how you may be feeling, then it's just not worth it. Or maybe your ways of thinking are just so different that you just do not agree on some topics no matter what. Don't engage in arguments with that person; you will never win. The person will not suddenly say, "oh yes, you are right," if they are argumentative and need to prove that they are right. As hard as it is, just let it go. No one wins in this scenario. You can argue for a long time with no positive result. So once the disagreement has begun, instead of going back and forth and arguing your side, just try to end the argument with "okay, well, I don't see it that way" or "I guess we'll just have to disagree about it." There is no point in arguing your side with some people. It will only make you upset, and you lose either way.

Some people will find ways to make you feel guilty. When you are going through a difficult time, there will be that person that finds a way to make it about them and may actually get you to feel bad for them when you were the one struggling. Learn to spot that behavior. Maybe you are having a difficult time with a sick loved one, and you have that difficult person that is upset that you are not going out or that you have not been calling them often enough. It is difficult for some people to put themselves in your shoes. They are focused on how they feel and may try to make you feel bad without thinking about your feelings. It's not fair, but that is how some people are. Don't apologize, and don't argue. You don't need to accept their blame or their guilt either. They may be upset or disappointed about something, but it does not mean you have done anything wrong. You can acknowledge their feelings without accepting their blame. Sometimes people can be persuasive and make us feel like we have done something wrong when we haven't. We feel enough guilt in our lives that we do not need to add any more guilt than we already have.

You can give someone everything you have and bend over backward for them, and it still won't be enough for them. These are the takers some of us have in our lives. They may ask you for favors and expect things from you. You may give in and do a lot for these people with little appreciation. You may still be asked to do more and more for them with little appreciation. Then, when you say that you cannot do a favor for them, the person gets upset with you. Even though you say no to doing a favor, these people may still get upset. It's okay to say no to things. You don't need to explain things to people. You don't have to explain your reason for not doing things. You are allowed to pass on things. I know some people will want a reason. Why? Why can't you do this for me? Why can't you go out tonight? Why can't you lend me money? They will try to get you to feel guilty enough to change your answer. You don't need to explain. You just can't today, and that's okay.

Unfortunately, some people are just annoying. Don't take it personally, and don't let it get to you. Some people cannot help having annoying personalities. That is just who they are. It's not even really their fault. I have more compassion for these people because you are usually not the only one who finds them annoying. They may have difficulty meeting friends or keeping friends due to their personalities. Remember, it has nothing to do with you. It's just who they are. You may not like them very much but try to have compassion for them.

I worked with another nurse on a hospital unit many years ago. She was often irritable, and I felt she was often rude to me. One day we were in the medication room together and she seemed especially moody. She threw her things on the counter and let out a big sigh. I decided that I needed to say something since she often made me feel uncomfortable. I asked her if I had done something or said something that upset her. At this moment, she gave me a perplexed look and said, "No. I just hate this place." Her attitude had absolutely nothing to do with me. It was nothing personal. I believe that my confronting her helped her realize the attitude she was bringing to work because her rude behavior decreased significantly.

"The truth is the way other people treat us isn't about us- it's about them and their own struggles, insecurities, and limitations. You don't have to allow their judgment to become your truth" Danielle Koepke.

Points to consider

- Don't let someone else's behavior influence your behavior.
- Don't engage with people that want to argue.
- Some people will continuously ask for things from you and offer little appreciation in return. They will continue to ask for things and make you feel guilty
- when you cannot do things for them. No matter how much you do, it will never be enough for some people, and they will not be satisfied.
- You are allowed to say no.
- Some people are annoying to everyone, so try not to take it personally.

The World

So many people get overwhelmed and feel helpless about things in our world. We cannot fix the whole world, but we can do something to make a change in it. When you feel bad about the state of the world, find something small that you can do to help make it better. If you feel bad about hunger or poverty, volunteer at a soup kitchen or donate food. These things we can do help us feel better about these large issues. If animals in shelters make you sad, donate needed items to your local shelters and offer help. Don't take the world's problems and put them on your shoulders. It's too overwhelming. But there are things you can do that helps and can be satisfying. Even though your change may seem small, it still counts, making the world a better place. I believe that if we all made small changes, those small changes would lead to a significant change. Small things can really change our world if enough people make them.

If watching the news depresses you or stresses you out, turn off the television. I interact with patients who get so upset by the news they are hearing, and it brings down their mood and makes them feel frustrated daily. I get the desire to be aware of current events, yet sometimes setting a limit can benefit your mental health. The ability to stream updated news all day everyday can be too much. If you are interested in looking at the news, try to limit the amount of time you are watching or reading the news so as not to feel too overwhelmed by it.

Points to considers

➢ Do not take the world's problems and put them on your shoulders.

➢ Making small changes still has a positive effect on the outside world.

➢ Don't spend too much time watching the news if it brings you down.

Maintaining Balance

Gratitude

One of the most inspirational people I have ever met was a patient I was treating while working as a medical-surgical nurse. I was sent to a surgical floor for my overnight shift. At the beginning of my shift, I reviewed my patient charts. I was caring for a male patient in his 60s that had been in the hospital for about four months. He suffered trauma after being partially run over by a truck. He had crushing injuries on the right side of his body that left his right leg paralyzed and part of his pelvis shattered. He had undergone several surgeries during his four months at the hospital.

After everything this patient had endured and needing to stay at the hospital for a long time, I expected him to need much care. I also thought he was going through a difficult time, and his mood may be low. I was surprised to see a gentleman sitting up in his hospital bed reading the newspaper. He looked my way with a pleasant smile. I introduced myself, and we spoke about his care. He told me how he tries to complete all his daily tasks independently, and he would contact me if he needed any help with them. He requested a bin of warm water to clean himself up.

We spoke throughout my shift, and he told me how he was very active before his accident. He was sure one of the reasons he survived was due to being in such great shape. He was engaged in whatever physical activities he could while in his hospital bed. I'm sure doing physical activity was painful at times for this man. But he started telling me about all the activities he would like to do once he leaves the hospital. Even knowing he would probably never walk again; he was working so hard to reach his highest level of activity and mobility. This man was so hopeful for his future. Through all the pain and struggles he endured; he was happy to be alive. He inspired me so much without even being aware of it. This experience is something that I have looked back on. It has made me think that limitations are not dead ends; they are only hurdles.

Feeling grateful for what we have takes practice initially if we are not used to it. It's important to recognize all of the things we are grateful for in our lives. When you are happy with the things you have instead of wanting something different, it helps you feel fulfilled and happy. As bad as you may have it, there is usually someone who has it worse. Sometimes, it is not easy to look at life in this way. I hear many tragic stories of suffering, and sometimes we just need to feel sad about our situation and cry about it. We can't always just think, "well, this terrible situation could be worse; let me just move on and be grateful for that." I know; we are only human. It's important to have your feelings, including sadness or anger. I encourage people to feel those feelings and experience them but not focus on the sad feelings hour after hour and day after day. At some point, we also need to focus on the good things happening in our lives.

When you begin to practice gratitude, you feel better about your life and what you have. There are gratitude journals out there that can be helpful when starting this practice. Just saying a few things that you were grateful for that day can be a step in the right direction. For example, if you are healthy, be grateful for feeling healthy. If you are financially stable, feel grateful for that. If you have supportive and loving people, be grateful for that. Do not take anything for granted.

Points to consider
- There is always something to be grateful for.
- Feeling grateful may take practice.

Coping

It's important to have healthy coping skills. Sometimes I ask my patients what makes them feel better and how they cope with having a bad day. We need ways of coping with our stress. I encourage people to find a hobby. Any kind of hobby that you enjoy will do. Having something that you enjoy is important. Many people tell me they are not "hobby people." Maybe you do not enjoy crafting, but maybe you like biking or hiking. The list of hobbies is long, and it would be worthwhile to explore different hobbies. At least try to find things that you may enjoy. Maybe you will enjoy reading, painting, drawing, journaling, sewing, exercising, learning to play an instrument, organizing, caring for a pet, doing makeup, cleaning, cooking, doing puzzles, practicing calligraphy, gardening, golfing, or listening to music. There are countless instructional videos online that you can try for any interest. Having a hobby can give you something to look forward to or something you can improve on over time.

Get out your thoughts. If you can, speak to someone about them. If you can't speak to anyone, write them out. Journaling can be helpful. When you are consumed by a thought, and you write it down it can be helpful to have the thought outside of you. Even if you are not writing in a typical journal and are just writing your thoughts on a scrap piece of paper, it can be helpful too. You can even throw away the paper once you are done. This may decrease the overthinking. Sometimes when we write things out, it changes our perspective. It may not look as overwhelming on paper as it felt when it was in your mind.

Writing to-do lists can be helpful when feeling overwhelmed as well. If you go to the grocery store without a list, you may have to keep repeating things you need in your mind. For example, repeating "I need bread, milk, and eggs." You may repeat this thought before leaving the house when you get in the car when you reach the supermarket, and then when you are walking down the aisles. It would be much easier just to write the items you need down so that you don't have to think about them repeatedly. This principle applies when thinking about the tasks we need to do. You may be thinking, "today, I need to do x, y, and z." You may continuously tell yourself what you hope to accomplish in the day. This can be overwhelming, and you may worry about forgetting something. When you write these things down, it can be easier to focus on one task at a time, and you may feel less overwhelmed.

Practice mindfulness. Be present. Learn to meditate. Meditating can be a good coping skill once you get the hang of it. Even if you start with two minutes per day, then increase to three minutes, then four, then five, etc. I like to practice visual meditations, such as picturing yourself in a peaceful environment and imagining the sounds of things you may see there. Sometimes I enjoy repeating a positive mantra and focusing on it during meditation. It can be helpful to use your breath during meditation as well. Practice exhaling all the negative energy and negative thoughts away from you and inhaling all of the positive and loving energy from the world on every inhale.

It can be rewarding when you find a practice that works for you. A few minutes of meditation per day can help clear your mind for the rest of the day. You may not find meditation helpful initially, but give it time, and you will see the reward. You may want to try practicing being more mindful or present in an active way, such as practicing a puzzle or going for a walk and trying to quiet your mind while completing these activities. This may help you when getting started on quieting your mind. Meditating is not for everyone, and if you are having difficulty and getting frustrated, take a break and try coming back to it at another time.

What do you enjoy? Do you spend any time doing it? I often ask my patients what they enjoy doing. Some of them say nothing. Some patients give me a list of things they enjoy that they have not done in days or weeks. If you want to feel good, it's important to regularly do things you enjoy. I know life is busy, and we do not all have time to go to a sporting event or go on vacation. Having something that you enjoy that does not take much time or is not expensive is a great tool. Maybe you enjoy taking a walk, visiting a park, playing a board game, or bathing. If you spend

Living in balance

your life going week to week without having anything you enjoy, the road to happiness will be much longer. If you need to look at your schedule and schedule something that you enjoy once every week, maybe that would be a good start. Usually, it is helpful to plan these things to make sure they happen.

Sometimes, when we feel down or depressed, we just don't want to go out or do anything. What's the alternative to not going to the gym or not going out with friends? Staying home and feeling bad about yourself or feeling lonely. This is when you need to force yourself to do something. I know it's not easy. It's easier to just lie under the covers, but this will only keep you stuck in a dark place and feeling bad. Maybe you won't go out every time you are invited, but if you can occasionally push yourself out of your comfort zone and get out there, it's a start. Ask yourself, if I don't do this, what will I be doing instead? If you do not have a healthy alternative, then the truth is that you don't have an alternative. You probably won't regret getting out from under the covers but will likely regret staying under them.

It is good to have some things you can do when you have an especially bad day. Having things that you know help you to feel better in advance is a helpful tool. Make a list for yourself that explains what you can do on a bad day. Some of these things may be going for a walk, talking to a friend, or listening to music. If you are having a bad day and do not have a plan of helpful things, you may rely on negative coping skills to feel better. It's hard to remember what makes us feel good when we are in a low place. Negative coping skills often make us feel better for a short period and usually make us feel worse later. These coping skills may be overspending, drinking alcohol, or self-harm, to name a few. They are not helpful. Negative coping skills do not add anything of value. They only take away from your true happiness. People get so used to using negative coping skills that they don't realize how much unhappiness the negative coping skills actually bring them. They sometimes say, "it's the only thing that makes me feel better," but it only makes them feel worse in the long run.

Living in balance

Points to consider

- Having interests or hobbies can be very beneficial.
- Write out your thoughts when overthinking.
- Practice being in the moment.
- Make plans to do things you enjoy.
- We can plan things that we enjoy that are inexpensive.
- Have things you can do when you are feeling down or are having a bad day.
- Negative coping skills usually make us feel worse later on.

Goal Setting

I can't stress the importance of setting goals. Every one of us can benefit from having goals. Have something to work on. Even if you have attained your biggest goals, it helps to have another goal to reach for. Many successful people have goals they are striving for. Goals can be anything big or small. Goals can be related to many things, including jobs, finances, health, relaxation, fitness, nutrition, relationships, or art. I can go on, but I think you get the point. I think it's helpful to have a few goals in different areas. Having a goal related to taking care of your body and finances and relaxation, for instance. It's good always to have something you are working on. Even if you want to floss more often or read more often, no goal is too big or small.

It is good to have big goals, but sometimes these can be overwhelming. So take your big goals and break them up into smaller goals. For example, if a goal is going back to school to complete a bachelor's degree, this goal may be overwhelming and should be broken down into smaller goals to help make it more attainable. So to break down this goal, I would make a list like this:

Complete my bachelor's degree:

Look at schools in my area that I would like to apply to next month.

Choose 2-3 schools to apply to.

Apply to school number one.

Apply to school number two.

Apply to school number three.

Take your goals and focus one step at a time to achieve your goal. If you are already thinking about how hard school may be or how you will manage to get everything done, just focus on one step at a time. Don't think about all future steps; just think about step number one. Then step number two. One step at a time, and anything is possible. With every step completed, you are one step closer to reaching your goal, which is something to feel proud of. So often, people forget to celebrate their small accomplishments. They are looking at crossing the finish line without acknowledging all of the steps on the way. Without step number one, you won't make it to the finish line, so it's good to feel proud of all of the steps you have completed. Don't wait to celebrate until the end. Don't wait to feel accomplished until you finish the project. Be happy when you are halfway there or even a quarter of the way there.

Always have something you would like to work on. Have a goal for your health and have something to look forward to. Goals can even be trips. Maybe you can't afford a trip to Bali, but you can plan a day to go to the beach, picnic by a lake, or go to your nearest state park. Plan things that you would like to do or see and add them to your list of goals.

Points to consider

- ➢ Make short-term goals and long-term goals.
- ➢ Break down massive goals into smaller goals.
- ➢ Celebrate your small accomplishments.

Time Wasters

So many times, people want to make changes in their lives but don't. They make excuses, and one of them is feeling as though there is not enough time. We all have ways that we waste time in our days. What are your time wasters? We all have them. Suppose you want to start exercising more often but do not feel you have time; there is a way to make time. Again, suppose you don't exercise at all and start exercising for twenty minutes three times a week; that is still an improvement. Most of us have twenty minutes three times per week. Maybe you sleep a lot; maybe you look on your phone a lot; maybe you watch television every night.

We usually have pockets of time that we are spending on something. Look at how you spend your time and find your time wasters. Completing a log to look at what you spend your time on can be a helpful way to find out what your time wasters are. Try filling out the log below as you go about your day. Include everything you have actually done in your daily log. Most people are surprised when they realize what they indeed do with their time. Don't waste too much time on time wasters.

Living in balance

	Monday	Tuesday	Wednesday	Thursday	Friday	Saturday	Sunday
8-9 am							
9-10 am							
10-11 am							
11-12 pm							
12-1 pm							
1-2 pm							
2-3 pm							
3-4 pm							
4-5 pm							
5-6 pm							
6-7 pm							
7-8 pm							
8-9 pm							
9-10pm							

Take care of your things

Whether you live in a mansion or a basement apartment, it is important to take care of your things. Take care of your environment. It makes people feel better when their environment is cared for. Try to keep your things neat and clean. If your place is full of clutter and dirt, it will negatively affect your mood. I often hear people tell me that the state of their home is a stressor. This is stress that will always loom in the background. People feel much better after cleaning or organizing their space. So just have a system and keep your things neat. Try to spend at least 15 minutes each day cleaning up. Get rid of things that are no longer useful or wanted. What are you waiting for? When you take care of things, they last longer and stay in better condition. Instead of buying things repeatedly, care for the things you have.

Living in balance

I think living a simple life decreases stress. The more you have, the more there is to take care of, and the harder it is to keep things in order. The more you have, the more you may need to work. I see people that dislike their job yet need to work extra hours to support their lavish lifestyle. Of course, it's nice to have nice things but maintain balance. Don't have so many things that it increases your stress level and takes away from your overall happiness. Living below your means is less stressful than being in debt.

Be Kind

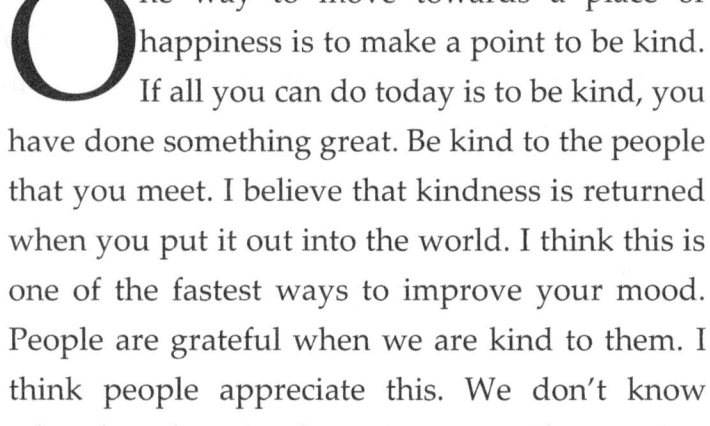

One way to move towards a place of happiness is to make a point to be kind. If all you can do today is to be kind, you have done something great. Be kind to the people that you meet. I believe that kindness is returned when you put it out into the world. I think this is one of the fastest ways to improve your mood. People are grateful when we are kind to them. I think people appreciate this. We don't know what the other people we interact with are going through, so being kind to someone can mean more than you know. Being kind benefits you in relationships, work, and everywhere you go.

One of my close friends had a young son that died. This was such a difficult time for her. I remember her explaining that she went to a local store to pick an outfit to bury her son in. While she was at the store, she looked around at the people around her going on with their normal day, not knowing that she was preparing for her son's funeral. You don't know if that person at the grocery store was recently diagnosed with a life-changing illness or if that person at the clothing store is picking an outfit to bury their son in. So it is so important to be kind to everyone you meet because they might be having one of the worst days of their lives, and your kindness might mean more than you know.

Sometimes it is easier to be kind to others than to be kind to ourselves. I find many people that struggle with this and are very critical of themselves. Being kind to yourself is just as important as being kind to everyone else. Sometimes, people's negative self-talk is worse than anything they would ever say to another person. This negative self-talk can come so easily. When engaging in negative self-talk, try to imagine you are talking to a friend. Is this something that you would say to a friend? If you look at yourself in the mirror and say you look disgusting, try to think if you would ever say that to someone you cared about. If it is not something, you would say to someone else, think of what you would say to someone you loved. If they looked bad in an outfit, you might say that it is not flattering; maybe something else would look better, but you would not say they look awful. If you make a mistake, you might engage in negative self-talk and say that you are a failure, but once again, if this was a friend, you may remind them that everyone makes mistakes. Look at your self-talk and try to remember to only say things to yourself that you would say to someone you cared about going through the same situation. This may take practice, but it will get easier over time. If you would like to be a kind person, remember that being kind to yourself is part of that. If you are engaging in negative self-talk, then remind yourself that you are working on being kind, including being kind to yourself.

Points to consider

- Be kind to others everywhere you go.
- Be kind to yourself.
- Look at your self-talk.
- Talk to yourself the way you would talk to someone else that you care about.

Be Helpful

Being helpful to others also helps us to feel good and happy. Of course, you do not want to go out of your way so that you feel overwhelmed or taken advantage of. But being helpful to others helps us feel as though we are making a positive impact on society and helps us feel good about ourselves. If you do not help others, you may become overly fixated on yourself. Everything may be about you, and you lose sight of what others are going through. You may start to lose a connection with others and care less and less about what other people are going through. Helping others makes you feel as though you are connected in a community with other people, which helps everyone, including you. As humans, we thrive when we work together in a community. Even if you see someone carrying many bags and open a door for them, it can make you feel good. We feel good about ourselves when we help others.

Being helpful reminds us that others are going through things too, and it helps us look outside of ourselves. This may also make it easier for you to ask for help when you need it. You may feel more comfortable knowing that everyone needs help sometimes, which is not bad.

Points to consider

➢ Helping others helps us all feel good.
➢ Helping others helps you to look outside of yourself.
➢ We all need help sometimes.

Keep Practicing

Happiness is not a straight path; there are highs and lows. Achieving happiness does not include crossing a finish line. To remain happy once you have achieved happiness, you will need to continue living your life in a way that helps keep you feeling happy. In life, we all have ups and downs. Once you feel happy, you will have a bad day again. That bad day will end, and you can feel happy again. Do not get too worried if you have a bad day.

It takes practice to sustain happiness. You will need to check in with how you are feeling and acknowledge when you feel angry, anxious, or sad. Pay attention to how the people around you make you feel. Do you have people in your life that help you to feel good, or do they bring you down? Remind yourself to work on your goals. Make plans for things you want to do or achieve. You also do not want to work so hard on wellness that you get overwhelmed. I have had people tell me that they created a checklist for feeling well and would meditate every morning and write in a gratitude journal every night, and they felt guilty if they skipped a day of doing this because they wanted to stay on top of their wellness plan. If doing wellness activities feels overwhelming, then take a step back. Start with simple things like eating well, sleeping well, getting some exercise, and being kind. If that is too much, just be kind and build from there when you are ready. Don't let wellness be another thing you have to do that makes you feel overwhelmed.

Use the tools you have learned in this book when times are getting hard. Look at your life section by section and think of where things may be out of balance. Are you maintaining balance in your body, mind, and relationships? If you stop caring for your physical self, work on this area. If you feel anxious and overwhelmed or have negative thoughts, focus on balance in your mind. I think the most critical areas for us are to maintain balance with our body and balance with our mind. If your body is feeling its best, it helps you feel good. If you have positive thoughts and manage your stressors and anxiety, it's hard for outside factors to bring you down. If you feel good about yourself and have positive thoughts, even when someone is being mean to you, it will not bother you very much. Other people will not be able to bring you down as much when you are maintaining balance in your thoughts.

If you are having difficulty with others and this brings you down, remember how to maintain balance in your relationships. Have you stopped using the tools to maintain balance, like goal setting or time management? These are the areas in our lives that bring us happiness and balance. If you are feeling out of balance, look at these areas and determine where to go from here, and the path to happiness can be found.

If you are in such a bad place that it is impossible to go through the sections in this book and apply them to your life, then maybe it is time for outside help. You may want to consult with a professional and work on a treatment plan. Sometimes people need to take medication to get better. There is nothing wrong with taking a medication if you need to improve your quality of life. Sometimes it seems impossible to begin the journey of feeling well, and that's when medication can be helpful. Once you feel better, it may be easier to apply the tools discussed in this book to help you feel your best. I believe there is always a way to make things better, so don't ever give up. I have treated people who were completely hopeless and ultimately found happiness, so I know that things can always get better.

Final points to consider

- It takes practice to sustain happiness.
- There will be ups and downs. There is no final goal.
- Do not let yourself feel overwhelmed with your wellness plan.
- If you are feeling bad, consider if you are maintaining balance in your body, mind, and with others. Then, look at where you may need to make improvements.
- No matter how bad things look, I believe the path to happiness can be found for every one of us.

About Kharis Publishing

Kharis Publishing, an imprint of Kharis Media LLC, is a leading Christian and inspirational book publisher based in Aurora, Chicago metropolitan area, Illinois. Kharis' dual mission is to give voice to under-represented writers (including women and first-time authors) and equip orphans in developing countries with literacy tools. That is why, for each book sold, the publisher channels some of the proceeds into providing books and computers for orphanages in developing countries so that these kids may learn to read, dream, and grow. For a limited time, Kharis Publishing is accepting unsolicited queries for nonfiction (Christian, self-help, memoirs, business, health and wellness) from qualified leaders, professionals, pastors, and ministers. Learn more at: [About Us - Kharis Publishing - Accepting Manuscript](#)

www.ingramcontent.com/pod-product-compliance
Lightning Source LLC
LaVergne TN
LVHW051524070426
835507LV00023B/3284